W9-DBX-759

EAGLES

Tim Harris

Grolier
an imprint of

www.scholastic.com/librarypublishing

Published 2008 by Grolier
An imprint of Scholastic Library Publishing
Old Sherman Turnpike, Danbury,
Connecticut 06816

For The Brown Reference Group plc
Project Editor: Jolyon Goddard
Copy-editors: Lesley Ellis, Lisa Hughes,
    Wendy Horobin
Picture Researcher: Clare Newman
Designers: Jeni Child, Lynne Ross,
    Sarah Williams
Managing Editor: Bridget Giles

Volume ISBN-13: 978-0-7172-6222-9
Volume ISBN-10: 0-7172-6222-7

**Library of Congress
Cataloging-in-Publication Data**

Nature's children. Set 1.
    p. cm.
  Includes index.
  ISBN-13: 978-0-7172-8080-3
  ISBN-10: 0-7172-8080-2
  1. Animals--Encyclopedias, Juvenile.
  QL49.N38 2007
  590--dc22

                    2007018358

Printed and bound in China

Contents

FACT FILE: Eagles

Class	Birds (Aves)
Order	Birds of prey (Falconiformes)
Family	Hawks and eagles (Accipitridae)
Genera	Several worldwide
Species	More than 70 worldwide, including the bald eagle (*Haliaeetus leucocephalus*) and the golden eagle (*Aquila chrysaetos*)
World distribution	The bald eagle lives only in North America; golden eagles live in North and Central America, Asia, Europe, and North Africa
Habitat	Varies with species
Distinctive physical characteristics	Sharp, hooked beak; powerful legs and long, curved talons; large wingspan
Habits	Usually mate for life; active only during the day
Diet	Bald eagles eat mostly fish; golden eagles eat small and medium-sized mammals and birds

Introduction

An eagle is a bird of **prey**. A bird of prey is a bird
that eats other animals, alive or dead. Birds of
prey also include owls. Unlike owls, eagles hunt
during the daytime. Eagles are large, strong birds.
They have long broad wings that measure up
to 8 feet (2.5 m) from one tip to the other. With
their large wings, eagles are strong fliers. They
can **soar** for long periods without flapping.
Eagles have long legs, with a sharp claw, or
talon, on each toe. They have a powerful beak
with a hooked tip.

**A crested eagle
chick learns to
use its wings.**

A South African tawny eagle watches for prey from its perch.

A Symbol of Power

Eagles have long been regarded as birds of power and might. Some ancient cultures thought eagles were the only creatures that could look directly at the Sun. Others thought they carried away the souls of dead people. Eagles are also associated with warriors and have often been used as symbols for armies and warring groups.

The reasons for the eagle's reputation are not hard to see. Eagles are among the biggest, most fearless, and intelligent of all birds. Ancient Greek people believed that when gods visited Earth, they might take the form of an eagle. Roman, Russian, Austrian, and French emperors used the eagle as a symbol of their empire's power. Native Americans believed that eagle feathers were signs of strength and courage. The bald eagle is used as an emblem of the United States. It can be seen on stamps, the back of dollar coins, and on the Great Seal of the United States.

Around the World

There are more than 70 different kinds of eagles. Eagles live on all the world's continents apart from Antarctica. They live in many different **habitats**. Some eagles live in the vast grasslands of Africa and Central Asia. Other eagles hunt in the mountains and build their nests on cliff ledges. Many eagles make their homes in forests, where they build their nests in tall trees. Still other eagles go into cities to find food. Some eagles hunt for fish over lakes, rivers, and even the oceans, although the birds do not usually stray far from the coast.

There are two North American eagles: the bald eagle, which is the national bird of the United States, and the golden eagle. The bald eagle likes to live near water. But the golden eagle makes its home in remote mountain areas.

Bald eagles live all over North America.

9

The harpy eagle
is the largest
eagle. It lives in
the rain forests
of South America.

Big and Small

Eagles are the biggest birds of prey. Bald eagles and golden eagles are very large, but they are not the biggest eagles. That prize goes to the harpy eagle, which lives in South American rain forests. Everything about the harpy eagle is massive: its wings, talons, beak, weight—and its appetite. It weighs up to 20 pounds (9 kg). At the other end of the scale, the little eagle is one of the smallest eagles. An adult male little eagle weighs only about 1 pound (500 g). A single harpy eagle weighs the same as 20 little eagles!

Snake eagles are also small birds. They live in Africa, Asia, and Europe. As their name suggests, snake eagles eat mostly snakes, which they pounce on from above. These eagles have short, powerful toes with which they tightly grasp their writhing dinner.

Eagles and Hawks

Eagles and hawks are close relatives. They are alike in many ways. Both eagles and hawks have wings that are broad and long. They both have a broad tail and spend much of their time soaring around, high in the sky, without flapping their wings. Hawks and eagles have excellent eyesight and have sharp talons to firmly grasp their prey.

The main difference between hawks and eagles is size. North American eagles are at least twice as large as the biggest hawks. All hawks and eagles have large beaks, but an eagle's beak is much longer than a hawk's. If you are lucky enough to see an eagle up close, you will see that its beak is nearly as long as its head.

This hawk has the same piercing eye and sharp beak of an eagle.

A bald eagle
in flight.

14

Fantastic Feathers

Just like other birds, eagles have feathers that cover all of their body except for the beak and legs. Some of these feathers keep the birds warm, and some help them fly. The feathers covering the body are much smaller and not as strong as those on the eagle's wings and tail. The feathers on the wings and tail are tough enough to support the bird when it flies.

The wing feathers overlap one another. This forms a broad paddle strong enough to push down the air and push it back up again as the eagle flaps its wings.

Some birds have brightly colored feathers, but not eagles. Usually, their feathers are a shade of brown, gray, or black. Adult golden eagles are brown all over. Bald eagles are also brown. At a distance, a bald eagle's head looks bald, which gives the bird its name. But the bald eagle's head is actually covered in white feathers.

Light but Strong

The skeleton of an eagle—or any other bird, for that matter—is incredibly strong but amazingly light. Its lightness is one of the reasons that birds are able to fly. Even the heaviest of the eagles is less than one-tenth the weight of a man, though the eagle's wingspan is longer than the height of most grown men.

Birds are so light for their size because their bones are hollow. In fact, the skeleton of a bald eagle weighs only about half a pound (225 g).

Though an eagle's bones are hollow, they are still incredibly strong. Without strong bones, an eagle wouldn't be able to fly fast, attack prey animals, or carry heavy prey. Eagles can do all those things because **cross-ribs**, or struts, within the bones give them added strength. The struts are a bit like the steel bars that strengthen a bridge or a tall building.

A bald eagle carries
a fish off to eat.

A bald eagle spots prey and begins to dive.

Rulers of the Skies

An eagle's wings are very long and very wide. The wings are so big that they can keep the bird aloft, much like a hang glider. Thus an eagle can stay high in the sky without having to flap its wings very often. Flying without flapping is called soaring. It allows the eagle to hunt without using up much energy.

There is one problem, though: the eagle has to climb from the ground to its position high in the sky. There are two ways to do that. The eagle can beat its wings for several minutes, gradually climbing higher and higher. But that is hard work. Or the eagle can hitch a ride on a column of warm, rising air, called a **thermal**. Eagles often ride thermals on hot, sunny days. It's a clever way to save energy!

Eagles are not the fastest birds when they are on a level flight path. But when eagles dive they can reach a speed of about 100 miles per hour (160 km/h)!

Feathery Legs

It is rare for birds to have feathers on their legs, and most eagles do not. But one group of eagles has feathers that grow almost all the way down to their feet. From a distance these eagles look as though they are wearing boots! That is why the members of this group, which include the golden eagle, are called booted eagles.

Bald eagles don't have feathery legs. They often get their feet wet when they catch fish. It would be a nuisance if they had feathery legs because their legs would be wet most of the time.

The feathery legs of a golden eagle make the bird look as though it is wearing tall boots.

Eagles have powerful talons for piercing, gripping, and lifting their prey.

22

Feet and Talons

Unlike a human foot, an eagle's foot has four muscular toes that it uses for grasping things. They are widely spread, with three facing forward and one pointing back. The back toe is used like a thumb to hold prey securely while the eagle is flying. Each toe has a sharp, curved talon that can pierce fish scales or animal skin. A bald eagle would really struggle to hold a fish if it didn't have sharp claws. And a golden eagle would not be able to catch a rabbit if it could use only its beak. When eating, eagles hold their prey with their talons while they bite into the flesh.

While all eagles have very strong toes, they are not all exactly the same. Bald eagles have lumpy, bumpy toes that are good for holding slippery fish. Golden eagles have smoother toes.

Eagles walk on their toes, as do other birds. However, they are rarely seen walking on the ground. Usually they are perched in a tree or on a rock, their strong toes firmly gripping the surface. They also use their feet to carry twigs for their nest.

Eagle Eyes

You've probably heard the expression "eyes like a hawk," used to describe someone with amazing eyesight. Well, eagles also have excellent vision. They can see some prey from 2 miles (3 km) away. Not even the most sharp-sighted person can do that.

Because eagles have such good eyesight, they can spot their prey even when they are flying high over a forest, lake, or grassy mountainside. The animal they are hunting probably will not see the eagle until long after the bird has seen its meal.

Eagles' eyes face forward, and that helps them judge distances. That is very important. If an eagle could see a tasty rabbit but had no idea how far away it was, the eagle wouldn't stand much chance of making a kill.

Three Eyelids

On a windy day, have you ever had to close your eyes to keep dust from blowing into them? The air is full of tiny pieces of matter that have been picked up by the wind. If, like an eagle, you were flying at top speed, your eyes would soon get very dry and full of dust.

If an eagle's eyes were damaged, it would not be able to hunt for food. It would soon starve to death. But eagles don't need to worry. That's because they have a see-through eyelid on each eye. This third eyelid lies beneath the upper and lower eyelids. It slides sideways across the eye. This eyelid also cleans and moistens the eye and protects it from dust and other danger.

Like all eagles, Steller's sea eagle has amazing eyesight and a powerful beak.

What's for Dinner?

Even the smallest eagles are very fierce birds. They will attack any animal that might make a suitable meal. Snake eagles, for example, pounce on snakes from above. These birds then crush their prey's head before swallowing the animal whole.

Other eagles eat frogs, lizards, birds, and mammals such as ground squirrels, rabbits, marmots, and prairie dogs. The huge harpy eagle sometimes snatches monkeys from the tops of trees. The fish eagles, including the bald eagle, eat—you've guessed it—lots of fish. Sometimes, groups of bald eagles gather near rivers where salmon have come to lay their eggs. The salmon are weary and weak after a very long journey, so the eagles find it easy to catch them.

Some eagles eat **carrion**, which is an animal that is already dead. The tawny eagle chases and robs other birds of prey of their food! Golden eagles can carry up to 8 pounds (18 kg) of food when they are flying.

A tawny eagle takes a rest after catching its dinner.

29

Pellets are the coughed-up parts of animals that a bird of prey cannot digest. Pellets contain fur, bones, and feathers.

Pellets

Eagles are not that fussy about what they eat. They swallow chunks of fish, mammal, or bird without bothering to separate the meat from the bone, fur, feathers, scales, or fins.

The intestines are hollow tubelike structures in the body, through which food passes. An eagle's stomach and intestines contain powerful acids and other chemicals. These chemicals break down food into simpler chemicals that provide nutrition for the body. This process is called digestion. But even the acids cannot break down most bones, fur, and feathers. These things do not get beyond the eagle's stomach. Instead, they are passed back up to the bird's mouth, then coughed up as **pellets**.

Usually, the center of a pellet is made up of bits of bone or fish scales, wrapped in a coating of fur and feathers. By looking at what is in a pellet, a scientist can tell what the eagle has had to eat.

Pairing Up

Once they have paired up, a male and female bald eagle or golden eagle may remain together for the rest of their lives. That does not mean they do everything together. But it does mean that at the start of the breeding season—usually at the end of winter—they renew their relationship.

Before the male and female eagle raise a family, they put on a number of amazing flying **displays**. The displays are called courtship. Bald eagles perform cartwheels in the air, swoop up and down as if they are on an invisible roller-coaster, and chase each other. They also call loudly to each other.

Golden eagles do similar things. They pretend to attack one another and grab each other's talons. The male birds suddenly dive then swoop back up, a process they may repeat up to 20 times in a single display.

When courting,
bald eagles chase
each other.

33

Bald eagles build huge nests made of sticks, with an inner lining of soft leaves and moss.

34

Enormous Nests

Bald eagles eat mostly fish. So they build their nest near water, often in the top of a tall tree. A bald eagle's nest is the biggest nest of any bird living in North America. Most bald eagle's nests are 5 or 6 feet (1.5 or 2 m) across and 3 feet (1 m) thick. But they can be bigger than that. Golden eagles build a huge nest, too. Their nest is made of sticks and other plant material, and the center is lined with soft grass, leaves, and moss.

When eagles return to a nest they built in a previous year, they will probably have to make repairs. The lining will have to be replaced, and some sticks may have been blown out by winter storms. Nests that are used year after year grow bigger and bigger. Scientists found one nest that weighed nearly 6,000 pounds (2,700 kg), which is as heavy as a small pickup truck!

Mating and Eggs

Why do eagles make such a big nest? They need a place to protect their eggs and, later, their chicks. They also need an area big enough to stand on when feeding their young.

Building one big nest is hard enough, but golden eagles often make more than one. The eagles build their nest, or nests, in an area called their **territory**. It is a very important area. The birds scare off any other eagles that try to hunt there. That way, the eagles make sure they have enough food to feed themselves and their family, too.

After a male and female eagle have **mated**, the female lays eggs. Usually there are two eggs, laid a few days apart. Sometimes bald eagles lay three eggs, and golden eagles may lay as many as four. Bald eagles' eggs are dull white. Golden eagles' eggs are white with little reddish brown spots on them.

A golden eagle's egg is white with reddish brown blotches.

37

This golden eagle chick has plenty of food to eat.

Warm Eggs

For an eagle's eggs to **hatch**, they must be kept warm. That job is done mostly by female eagles. After about 35 days, the developing chick inside a bald eagle egg is strong enough to break out of its shell. It usually takes a little longer for a golden eagle chick to hatch.

Having a few days between laying each egg is helpful to parents. That is because then there is also a gap between the eggs hatching. Baby eagles, or **eaglets**, are hungry as soon as they hatch. For the first few days the parents have only one chick to feed. When the second eaglet hatches, their lives become busier still!

Hungry Eaglets

Chicks usually hatch in late spring or summer, when there's plenty of food for them. However, they can't feed themselves for a long time. Like a human baby, they have to be fed by their parents.

For a while, the father brings most of the food to the nest while the mother stays close to the small chicks. When the babies are a little older, both parents hunt for them. Bald eagles bring mostly fish for their young, and golden eagles bring mammals and birds. The chicks cannot eat big chunks of meat, so the adult eagles tear it up into small pieces. The oldest chick usually eats first. Gradually, the pieces of food that are fed to the eaglets get bigger and bigger.

Young eagles always seem to be hungry. They constantly call to their parents for more food. A newly hatched bald eaglet grows from about 3 ounces (90 g) when it hatches, to 9 to 11 pounds (4–5 kg) after about two months.

A bald eagle watches over its rapidly growing chicks.

A crested eagle
chick practices
flapping its wings.

Learning to Fly

When they first hatch, eaglets are covered in very soft gray feathers called **down**. These help keep the chicks warm. After four or five weeks, tougher feathers begin to grow. Then after six or seven weeks, the youngsters can feed themselves if food is left in the nest.

After seven weeks, young golden eagles start to leave the nest. As with babies learning to walk, some learn before others. If the nest is on a cliff ledge, the chick may simply be able to walk or hop out. Sometimes, the chick leaves the nest by falling! At 10 weeks, young golden eagles might make their first flight. Before they develop the courage to do that, they practice hopping up and down and flapping their wings. Young bald eagles can't walk out of their nest because it is high in a tree. They usually first fly when they are about 11 weeks old.

Leaving the Nest

Learning to fly is not easy, but once they can do it, young eagles are almost ready to leave home. Almost, but not quite. At first, they are not very good fliers. They are also not very good at catching their own dinner.

So the young birds practice, and they watch their parents. Practice makes perfect, and by the end of the summer, they have become skilled hunters. Once they have been flying for a month or two, it is time to leave the nest. Their parents know that if their offspring remain in their territory through the difficult months of winter, there won't be enough food to go around. So, once the young birds can take care of themselves, the parents make them leave the territory.

This short-toed eaglet will soon leave the nest.

A brown snake eagle shows off its impressive wing feathers.

Changing Feathers

Like all birds, eagles grow new feathers to replace their old ones every year. If they didn't do that, their feathers would simply wear out. They would become tattered, and the birds wouldn't be able to fly. When a bird replaces its feathers, the process is called **molting**.

Young golden eagles and bald eagles have brown feathers. They look very much alike. Young eagles need to molt several times. They will be four or five years old before they look like adults. Bald eagles grow the familiar white feathers on their head and neck. Golden eagles grow golden-brown feathers on their head. Brown snake eagles have brown feathers but with a paler underside.

Coming of Age

Even when they have grown their adult feathers, eagles may not be quite ready to pair up and raise a family. But usually that time is not far away. Between the ages of four and seven years, golden eagles and bald eagles are ready to do what their parents did before them: find a mate.

Adult eagles do not breed every year. Even when they do attempt to raise young, they sometimes fail. The weather may turn cold, so the eggs don't hatch. Or they may not be able to catch enough food to provide for their chicks. And often the young birds make it out of the nest but cannot survive the harsh winter.

However, if they are lucky, eagles may live to the grand old age of 25 years or more. And during this time, they are sure to raise several families of their own.

Words to Know

Carrion   The flesh of dead animals, eaten as food.

Cross-ribs   Bars within a bird's hollow bones. Cross-ribs strengthen the bones.

Displays   Showing-off behaviors that animals use to attract a mate or claim a territory.

Down   Very soft, fine feathers.

Eaglets   Baby eagles.

Habitats   Types of places where an animal or plant lives.

Hatch   To break out of an egg.

Mate   Come together to produce young animals.

Molting   To shed one set of feathers and replace them with a new set.

Pellets   Coughed-up parts of animals that a bird of prey cannot digest, or break down. Pellets usually include bones, fur, and feathers.

Prey   Animals hunted by another animal for food. A bird that hunts animals for food is often called a bird of prey.

Soar   To rise high in the sky by using air currents, not by beating the wings.

Talon   The claw of an eagle, hawk, owl, or other bird of prey.

Territory   Area that an animal or group of animals lives in and often defends from other animals of the same kind.

Thermal   A column of warm, rising air. Birds often ride on thermals to save energy.

Find Out More

Books

Douglas, L. G. *The Bald Eagle*. Danbury, Connecticut: Children's Press, 2003.

Merrick, P. *Eagles*. Mantako, Minnesota: The Child's World, Incorporated, 2006.

Penny, M. *Natural World: Golden Eagle*. London, UK: Hodder and Stoughton Children's Division, 2001.

Web sites

All About Eagles
www.eagles.org/all.html
Facts about several types of eagles.

All About the Bald Eagle
www.enchantedlearning.com/subjects/birds/info/Eagle.shtml
Information and a quiz about the bald eagle.

Index